Writing

HOW TO TURBOCHARGE YOUR SENTENCES FOR MAXIMUM IMPACT

Janet Cosgrove

Gould & Greene Publishing Co.

NEW YORK, NY

Copyright © 2016 by Janet Cosgrove

All rights reserved.

Published in The United States of America
by Gould & Greene Publishing Company

ISBN-13: 978-1520246000

ISBN-10: 1520246005

No part of this book may be reproduced in any form unless written permission is granted from the author or publisher. No electronic reproductions, information storage, or retrieval systems may be used or applied to any part of this book without written permission.

Due to the variable conditions, materials, and individual skills, the publisher, author, editor, translator, transcriber, and/or designer disclaim any liability for loss or injury resulting from the use or interpretation of any information presented in this publication. No liability is assumed for damages resulting from the use of the information contained herein.

Contents

Introduction 1

Getting Started: The Basics of Writing 3

Why Sentence Structure is Important 9

The Parts and Types of Sentences 22

How to Improve Your Writing Style 36

More Ways to Turbocharge Your Sentences 45

Some Additional Stylistic Tips 56

Conclusion 67

Answers to Quizzes 68

Dedicated to aspiring writers everywhere

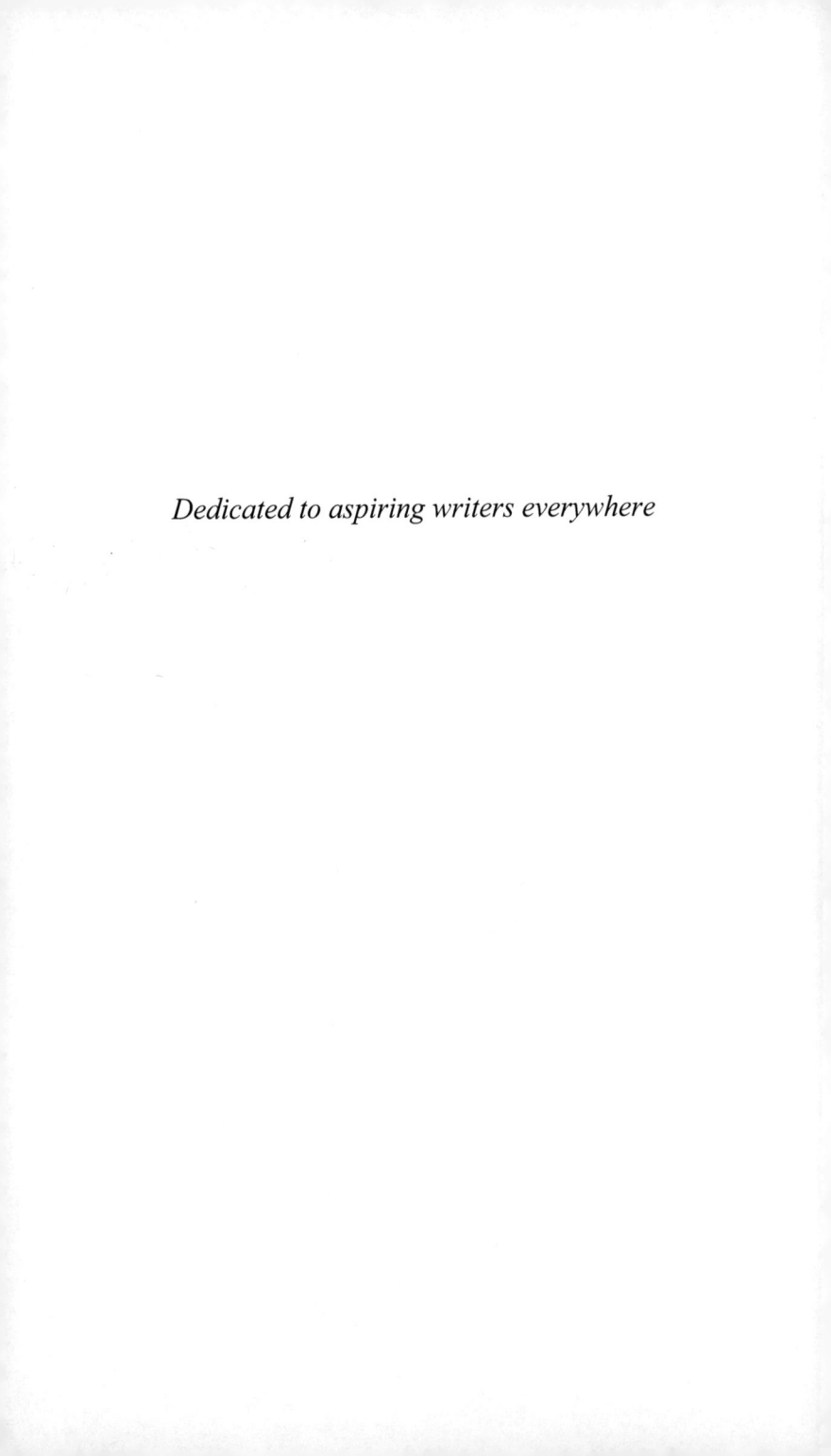

"There is nothing to writing. All you do is sit down at a typewriter and bleed."

—ERNEST HEMINGWAY

Introduction

Do you have to write on a regular basis but have difficulty getting your ideas across? Do you want to be able to better express your thoughts and influence others with your words?

If so, this guide was written for you.

The following pages are jam-packed with actionable information on how to take your writing to the next level.

Although you may enjoy seeing your words in print, you might find writing a challenge not because you lack enthusiasm, but because you have yet to discover how to write right—that is, how to express yourself in a concise, error-free, and persuasive way.

This shortcoming may not seem to be too much of a problem at first, but if your writing fails to captivate and reach others over the long term your credibility could be dealt a major blow. If you are a student, it will mean lower grades; if you are a businessperson, a failed proposal, a lost contract, or maybe even dismissal. In our ruthlessly competitive world, you ignore the development of your writing skills at your peril.

If you, like most people, struggle daily with your prose, there is nonetheless some good news: *You can improve your writing skills to deliver the knockout punch you need to achieve your educational and/or career goals.* How? By turbocharging your sentences for maximum clarity, energy, and impact.

This guide will help you master all the essential writing skills you need to boost your confidence and write like a true professional. Inside, you will learn how to infuse your sentences with vigor, weed out needless words, avoid embarrassing grammatical mistakes, and employ turns of phrase you never thought possible.

Most importantly, you will learn how to *write right*. Now, let's get started.

CHAPTER 1

Getting Started: The Basics of Writing

Before we can discuss specific strategies to help you craft turbocharged sentences, it is critical that we start with the basics of writing.

It goes without saying that writing is an important part of our daily lives. It facilitates communication, strengthens business relationships and bonds with family and friends, and helps society function. Furthermore, writing serves as the foundation for careers in journalism, public relations, marketing, sales, economics, and many other fields.

Writing is one of the most reliable and efficient means to track events in our daily lives, making it a key innovation in human evolution.

In many ways, our lives revolve around writing, and we could hardly function without it.

This compounds the importance of developing good writing skills. We must write well for our personal wellbeing, but also in a professional sense to meet the demands of educational institutions and the modern workplace.

To motivate you into implementing the writing right strategies covered in this guide, the following section discusses the benefits of good writing and why writing right is important.

Benefits of Writing

Your skill at writing can make the difference between your success or failure in relationships, business, and life in general. As a social being, there will be many instances where you need to communicate with others, argue your case, and influence crucial outcomes.

Although we employ mostly verbal and non-verbal communication in our daily lives, writing figures prominently in our social interactions. For instance, when updating your online social media profiles, you must write; when applying for a job or submitting a business proposal, you must also write. While most people today type down information for themselves or others using computers, the thought processes involved in writing remain the same as when the texts were written with pen or pencil and paper.

But writing is not just something people do out of obligation. Writing also provides less obvious benefits we should also think about:

Writing can be therapeutic

Sometimes it is necessary to speak your mind to make your point understood. You can do this orally, or through writing. But sometimes it is best to keep your thoughts to yourself. At such times writing down your grievances, doubts, regrets, hopes, and fears in a journal will help clear your mind and focus on what is important. You can then seek solutions and enjoy life more fully.

Writing helps you stockpile ideas

Human beings have great aspirations, and flashes of insight can come at any time. Everyone, for instance, has heard the story of Archimedes, who, while naked in his bathtub, shouted "Eureka!" when discovering the principle that bears his name. Committing your brilliant ideas to memory for later use is not so easy, however, because your mind is prone to forgetfulness. By writing your thoughts down, you can revisit your ideas, brainstorm, and modify earlier concepts as you deem fit. You can delve deeper and deeper into your original idea over time thanks to writing, an impossibility when you try to build on knowledge without written documentation.

Writing gives you an opportunity to exercise your mind

Through writing, you release pent-up creativity by stimulating the cognitive processes in your brain. Just like a muscle strengthened by weight training, the brain grows stronger with regular use. Through writing and the deep thinking associated with it, your brain remains sharp and active, preventing or slowing down the onset of diseases such as dementia or Alzheimer's.

Obviously, however, writing right is more than just putting words on a page; your writing must also be effective. Improving your writing skills will help highlight your intellectual and professional strengths, which in business settings will win over clients and boost your career prospects. In educational contexts, writing well will help you take high-quality lecture notes, craft outstanding essays, excel on exams, and enter the ranks of the top-performing students.

Taking It Further: Why You Need to Write Right

Some benefits of developing exceptional writing skills include the following:

1. By writing memos, letters, and procedures well, you will more smoothly manage your company operations. Through clear and persuasive writing, you can effectively communicate and promote workplace changes, or ask for increased financial compensation. Superb writing skills will help you clarify issues to colleagues, clients, and other third parties, avoiding the frustration and misunderstandings that arise from ineffectual writing.

2. You can promote goodwill for your company by sending well-written letters to customers with complaints, redressing their problems or explaining why you cannot meet their demands. Furthermore, if you have grievances or compliments about services or products you have purchased, writing a well-voiced and curated letter will see to it that your views are taken seriously.

Perhaps, as well, you might wish to write to your local government about an issue that is important to you. If you do so in a persuasive way, you could very well end up influencing public policies and impact the lives of people in your community.

3. Writing well will improve your reasoning skills in your daily life. Constant use of well thought-out and orderly sentences will alter your thought patterns in a positive way, helping you analyze different life situations effectively and develop your problem-solving skills.

With all these benefits, developing your writing skills is something you can ill afford to treat as an afterthought. It is essential that you find ways to enliven your writing, improve your sentence structure, sharpen your grammar, captivate readers, and communicate your point of view as convincingly as possible.

For a moment, think about what constitutes good writing. How can you inject vigor into your sentences? How can you make your sentences more readable and memorable? In a word, how can you turbocharge your sentences for maximum impact?

Undoubtedly, improving your writing skills will require a lot of hard work and patience. To develop your skills, you must develop a thorough understanding of sentence structures so you can constructively create fluid and meaningful sentences. To help you get started, the next chapter discusses the importance of sentence structure for effective writing.

CHAPTER 2

Why Sentence Structure is Important

Imagine you have just ordered a meal at a restaurant you are visiting for the first time. Now, imagine the waiter brings you a box of ingredients and utensils, drops them on your table, and comments, "Okay, there you are. You'll have to make it yourself. Sorry we don't have the recipe for you. You can figure it out. Anyway, that'll be $28.96. Here's the bill."

Of course, if the above situation were to happen the restaurant would quickly go out of business. What kind of enterprise would treat the customer with such little respect and make him or her do all the work?

As absurd as such a restaurant sounds, it is not unusual for unskilled writers to do something similar with readers. Rather than taking the time to organize their thoughts and present them in a cogent way, such writers throw disconnected ideas and information down on paper and hand the result to unsuspecting readers, expecting them to perform intellectual gymnastics to extract meaning from the jumbled mess before them.

Maybe you have suffered at the hands of such people—or have even been guilty of perpetuating such deeds yourself. However, as commonsense tells us, just putting down ideas and information is insufficient, especially if the way you express them is confusing. In simple terms, having great ideas and data is well and good, but organizing everything in a coherent manner is what matters most.

As another example, think of watching a well-choreographed salsa dance and its carefully synchronized movements. The dancers' steps move seamlessly in tandem with the beat—it is as if the dancers and music are one. Think also about the dancers' colorful costumes and how they further add to the display of artistry before you. What could be more elegant and impressive? Will not the memory of the dance linger in your mind for years to come?

Your writing should resemble a well-choreographed dance. To "dance" well, you must arrange your thoughts into meaningful, clear, and cohesive passages. To do otherwise will leave your audience disappointed. The flow and style of your writing, embodied in the rhythm and imagery of your sentences, also leave an indelible impression, as does your choice of vocabulary. Just like a dancer prepares for a show in front of an audience, a skilled writer crafts his or her words with care and respect for the reader.

... At least, that is how it should be.

Unfortunately, many writers lack the training or knowledge needed to dazzle readers or at least convey a clear and simple message. One of the main reasons they fall short is they do not understand basic sentence structure. Proper structure, however, is essential not only for you to be understood but also to engage with readers and leave a good impression. Furthermore, with well-written sentences, you can then construct proper paragraphs. Without solid sentences as a foundation, cohesive and effective paragraphs will elude even the best-intentioned writer.

Let us examine in more detail why proper sentence structure is so important for writing.

Sentence Structure: Its Place in Writing

Sentence structure is what orients your writing. Beyond the logic and precision of words, employing effective sentence structure adds panache to your writing. Some of the benefits of proper sentence structure include the following:

1. Proper sentence structure enables you to use modifiers effectively.

Normally, a modifier provides description in a sentence. A modifier can be a clause, a phrase, or a word and, depending on where you place it within a sentence, it may lead to clarity or confusion. The following tips can help you use modifiers effectively:

a. Carefully use modifiers to transfer an image or picture you have in your mind to your readers.

For instance, consider the following sentence:

"Peter lifted the box."

The sentence is fine, but can be improved by adding modifiers such as in this rewrite:

"Peter lifted the heavy box overflowing with Christmas gifts."

The word *heavy* (an adjective) is a modifier and the clause *overflowing with Christmas gifts* is also a modifier. These modifiers make the sentence more vivid, helping the reader imagine what Peter was lifting.

b. Always place a modifier next to the word it describes.

This helps you avoid confusing the reader. Remember, depending on where you place a modifier, the same word can lend different meanings to a sentence.

For example, consider the use of the word just in the following sentences.

"Terry just nodded to Jones as she came in."

This sentence may mean that Terry did not do any other thing apart from nodding. Next, consider this version:

"Terry nodded to Jones just as she came in."

Here, Terry nodded when she entered. Now, look at the sentence with "just" in yet another position:

"Terry nodded just to Jones as she came in."

In this case, Terry did not nod to anyone except Jones.

c. Avoid misplaced modifiers.

Words such as *only*, *almost*, *simply*, *exactly*, *merely*, *scarcely*, etc. are easy to misplace and can end up making your writing sound confused, awkward, or downright illogical. Consider the following:

> "The tailor almost bought all the crochet hooks."

This sentence could mean the tailor did not buy the hooks but nearly did. If the author's true meaning was that the tailor bought many hooks (but not all of them), the sentence should read:

> "The tailor bought almost all the crotchet hooks."

d. Avoid dangling modifiers.

Consider this sentence:

> "When just four years old, Tony's grandpa taught Tony ballet."

It contains a dangling modifier as it suggests Tony's grandpa was four years old when he taught Tony ballet. The sentence should read:

> "When just four years old, Tony learned ballet from his grandfather."

2. Employing good sentence structure will help you eliminate fragments and run-on sentences.

Fragments are incomplete sentences unattached to clauses, as in the following example:

> "Eating fruits and vegetables daily is important. Getting all the nutrients you need."

"Getting all the nutrients you need" is a fragment. It should be combined with the first sentence to read:

> "Eating fruits and vegetables daily is important for getting all the micronutrients you need."

A true sentence, unlike a fragment, should contain a complete idea.

Likewise, avoid joining two or more independent clauses without applying appropriate conjunctions or punctuation; otherwise, you risk having run-on sentences. For example, consider:

> "Adriano always knew his way around the city center this is something he could always rely on."

This sentence contains two clauses. However, it is difficult to distinguish the two, interfering with the flow of the sentence. Applying proper punctuation results in the following:

> "Adriano always knew his way around the city center; this is something he could always rely on."

The good news is that fragments and run-on sentences are easy to fix. All you must do is add missing parts to fix fragments and split run-on sentences into two sentences.

---

3. Good sentence structure helps you avoid overusing the passive voice.

The passive voice often makes sentences hard to follow. Normally, it emphasizes the person or object receiving an action, as in:

> "The minutes were written by Trevor."

This is an example of the passive voice because "the minutes" is emphasized at the beginning of the sentence when Trevor is the one who performed the action of writing. The reader will not have too much difficulty understanding that

Trevor was responsible for the minutes, but the sentence is too wordy and lacks punch.

We can rewrite the same sentence in the active voice as:

> "Trevor wrote the minutes."

In this case, the sentence is more concise and straightforward. The active voice also helps engage the reader as it is more vigorous than the passive voice.

While the passive voice can be useful for describing processes and procedures, particularly in science (e.g., "One milligram of sodium was added to the solution."), one major weak point, in addition to adding unnecessary words to sentences, is that it can be unclear who is responsible for an action. Consider this sentence:

> "Thousands of employees were laid off last financial quarter."

In this example, those responsible for the action are not identified. This use of grammar could be an effort to deceive readers or minimize responsibility for a negative action. A revised version of the sentence in the active voice reads:

> "XYZ Company laid off thousands of employees last financial quarter."

In the second example, it is clear who was responsible for the layoffs.

How can you improve your sentence structure? First, you must understand sentence types, which are discussed in the next chapter. Before that, however, brace yourself for an exercise that will jog your memory and determine if you have grasped the ideas discussed in Chapter 2.

Quiz 1

1. Identify the modifier(s) in the following sentence:

> *Poor Tracy, who just wanted a quick meal to get through her two-hour botany lab, shrieked and dropped her spoon on the floor as a spider crawled out from under her lunch box.*

2. Identify the modifier(s) in the following sentence:

> *She strolled down the avenue with a jaunty, defiant step, as if daring passersby to intrude upon her cheerful mood.*

3. Correct the following sentence:

> *Once corrected and rewritten, he excelled.*

4. Rewrite the following sentence to eliminate the dangling modifier:

> *After frying for 30 minutes, we turned the cooker off.*

5. Which sentence makes logical sense?

a. Filling the shopping basket with bottled water and canned foods, our tornado preparation was eventually complete.

b. Filling the shopping basket with bottled water and canned foods, we eventually completed our tornado preparation.

c. Filling the shopping basket with bottled water and canned foods, the completion of our tornado preparation relieved our anxiety.

6. Select the sentence that makes logical sense:

    a. Marion rode her squeaky, rusty bike to the park.

    b. Squeaky with rust, Marion rode her bike to the park.

    c. Marion rode her bike to the park which was squeaky with rust.

7. Read the sentence below and determine if it has a dangling or misplaced modifier.

    Emily was delighted when the tutor returned her Mathematics test with an ear-to-ear grin.

8. Rewrite the following sentences using the active voice:

    a. He was found at the beach.

b. The culprits were apprehended by the police.

c. By whom were you taught French?

d. The revolution was started by people from the South.

9. Determine if the following excerpt has a fragment:

As Christmas draws nearer, I find myself reminiscing about my childhood days of fun-filled family get-togethers and sing-alongs. Thinking about this makes me happy.

10. Read the following sentence and correct it where necessary:

The meeting begins at 4:20 pm make sure you arrive early.

CHAPTER 3

The Parts and Types of Sentences

As an avid reader, you will come across many types of sentences. Can you identify them? Can you effectively apply each one to your own writing?

Employing different types of sentences, whether in business, literary or academic writing, can invigorate and make your prose easier and more enjoyable to read. Indeed, professional writers all know that varying the length and structure of sentences is a key strategy to avoid boring readers and maintain their rapt attention. It also provides a means to emphasize select ideas.

The Parts of Sentences

Clauses are groups of words that contain both verbs (indicating actions) and subjects (nouns). Sometimes the subject is replaceable with a noun phrase, while the verb is replaceable with a verb phrase. Clauses are also categorizable as independent and dependent clauses.

An *independent clause* is a complete sentence. It is a main clause and can stand alone as a sentence. An example of an independent clause is the following:

"Pete tore the paper bag."

A *subordinate* or *dependent clause*, however, cannot stand alone as a sentence since it does not express a full thought.

Dependent clauses are normally introduced by subordinating conjunctions such as *what, because, while, although, which, if, who*, etc. The three types of dependent clauses are *noun clauses, adjective clauses,* and *adverb clauses*.

1. Noun clauses

These clauses function as predicate nominatives, subjects, objects of prepositions, and objects. They also serve as nouns in the following sentences:

"Tomorrow you can do whatever you want."
—object

"Whoever ate that cookie is in big trouble."
—subject

2. Adjective clauses

These function as adjectives and they start with a relative pronoun. Pronouns normally take the place of nouns, mostly direct preceding nouns, as in the following:

"Few people are familiar with the Chinese alligator, which is found in eastern China."

"This is the elementary school where I attended Grades 1 and 2."

You may use commas around adjective clauses to show that the information is not significant for the flow of the sentence. However, if you do not use commas, it means that the information is important. For example, consider:

"The goat that is in the pasture belongs to Kate."

This implies that among all the goats on a farm, Kate owns the one in the pasture. When you introduce commas, the sentence becomes:

"The goat, which is in the pasture, belongs to Kate."

This means that the farm has only one goat and you are only giving non-essential information by pointing out that it is in the pasture.

Note that when you use the word "that" without commas you introduce an essential clause. However, when you use "which" with commas you introduce non-essential clauses. Furthermore, a pronoun (like that and which) always refers to one noun. Avoid the incorrect usage of "which." For instance, it is wrong to say:

> "Your papers must be submitted before the deadline, <u>which</u> is one way for you to excel as a student."

The word "which" makes the sentence ambiguous because it may refer to the papers or deadline. Instead, say:

> "One way for you to excel as a student is to submit your papers before the deadline."

3. Adverb clauses

Adverb clauses modify adjectives, verbs, or adverbs and function as adverbs in a sentence. Consider these two example sentences:

> "Let's go outside and cheer <u>when the Governor arrives</u>."

> "Don't leave <u>until she comes back</u>."

Remember, all your sentences must have at least one independent clause. An independent clause is an essential element without which your sentence becomes a fragment. Fragments are a major error in writing.

Types of Sentences

As discussed earlier, constituent clauses determine the various types of sentences. The three types of sentences are: (1) simple sentences; (2) compound sentences; and (3) complex sentences.

1. Simple sentences

A simple sentence is also an independent clause because it consists of one main clause. It expresses a single idea and has one subject–verb combination, although it may have more than one element as the subject (compound subject).

Consider the following examples:

"Paul is going home."

"The government and the union held peaceful negotiations."

In the second case, the subject is compound (the government and the union).

Sometimes, simple sentences may also have compound verb constructions. Here is an example:

> "She worked hard and performed very well."

Note that commas are not used in simple sentences. However, compound verbs, compound subjects, and prepositional phrases may help lengthen simple sentences. Avoid too many simple sentences or your writing will become "choppy"—or consist of paragraphs with short, childlike sentences that make for dull, lackluster reading.

2. Compound sentences

Sometimes you may want to combine two main clauses to make a single sentence. By using coordinating conjunctions (like *but*, *and*, *or*, *for*, *yet*, *nor*) to combine these two clauses, you get a compound sentence.

Here are examples:

> "They lost the match, but won the League cup."

> "I looked for Steve and Ruby at the Railway station, but they reached the station before dusk and left on the train just as I arrived."

In a sentence, coordinating conjunctions can indicate a relationship between two independent clauses. Sometimes, this relationship never comes out as such. For instance, the word "and" just adds an independent clause to another and may not show any logical relationship between the two parts of a sentence. Therefore, your writing will be weak if you use too many such sentences.

3. Complex sentences

A complex sentence consists of one main clause as well as one or even several subordinate clauses. In this case, the subordinate clause may precede the main clause or vice versa.

Here are two examples:

> "When they reached home, they held lengthy discussions on how to strengthen trade relations between Peru and Paraguay."

> "They held lengthy discussions on how to strengthen trade relations between Peru and Paraguay when they reached home."

Usually, the main parts in a complex sentence have clearer and more specific relationships. For instance, by using the word "before" your reader learns that one thing precedes another. Similarly, the word "although" may also reveal an intricate connection than just using the coordinating conjunction "and." As a result, complex sentences more effectively communicate your ideas than compound sentences do.

Try to spice up your writing from time to time with a periodic sentence. This is a complex sentence that begins with a subordinate clause and ends with a main clause, as such:

> "While he waited at the canteen, Chris realized that Susan was late."

In such a sentence, the reader finds the full thought last. The first part of the sentence builds up to the whole meaning located at the end. A subtle degree of suspense can make periodic sentences highly effective, when the situation calls for such use.

Even though sentences beginning with the coordinating conjunctions *and* and *but* stand out, you should use them sparingly. However, your sentences can start with *because* if the sentences are complete.

Common Errors

While you may seek to make your writing as appealing as possible, your sentences can still have problems. Apart from fragments and run-ons, other common errors include: (1) loose sentences; (2) choppy sentences; (3) faulty parallelism; and (4) excessive subordination.

1. Loose sentences

A loose sentence occurs when phrases or modifying clauses follow a main clause. The additional phrases seek to elaborate the main idea in the main clause. Sometimes, weak sentence construction may result in a loose sentence, especially if you add modifying clauses in random order.

Consider the following example:

> "In the event that we're contracted, we must be ready by next summer with the required equipment and personnel to do the job, hence with this end in mind a brainstorming meeting, which all members of the production team are expected to attend, is scheduled after your vacation."

This passage is difficult to understand. We can improve it by breaking it up into several sentences instead of using one unwieldy sentence.

In addition, using too many "and" connectives instead of appropriate conjunctions may make your sentences "loose." Here is an example of this error:

> "Dave had a knee problem, and he stopped jogging."

We can rewrite this sentence using "so" instead of "and" to read:

"Dave had a knee problem, so he stopped jogging."

2. Choppy sentences

Choppy sentences occur when you successively use short sentences without transitionally linking them. Consider the following:

"The results are inconsistent. The process is flawed. Let's talk to Maria. We'll ask her to review the process."

You could change the passage to read:

"We'll ask Maria to review the process since it produced inconsistent results."

3. Faulty parallelism

Parallelism, when employed correctly, is useful for emphasis and effect. When used incorrectly, the result is called "faulty parallelism." In the former case, sequential sentence parts follow the same structural or grammatical principle; in the latter, they do not. To understand what exactly is meant by parallelism, look at the following sentences:

"I like reading, jogging, and to dance."

"I like reading, jogging, and dancing."

The first sentence contains faulty parallelism. The second sentence employs parallelism correctly. Using parallel structure introduces rhythm to your writing and can sound especially impressive in speeches.

4. Excessive subordination

Excessive subordination occurs when a sentence consists of a series of clauses each subordinating a preceding one. You can correct this error by turning some of the subordinate clauses into modifying phrases or breaking the sentence into two or more sentences.

Here is an example:

> "Dawn believed that she was prepared but she failed the examination meaning she had to repeat the course before she could graduate which she didn't want to do because it would conflict with her new appointment."

This sentence is cumbersome and difficult to understand. You can revise it as follows:

> "Dawn believed that she was prepared, but she failed the examination. She would now have to repeat the course before she could graduate. This was an outcome she desperately wanted to avoid, since it would conflict with her new appointment."

Notice how much better the second example flows? To avoid excessive subordination, review your work to single out parts that need revision, just like was done above.

Congratulations for coming this far! While learning how to turbocharge your sentences takes lots of time, it is well worth the effort. Next, we will explore how to improve your writing to attract and keep readers' attention.

Before that, here is an exercise to test what you have learned so far.

Quiz 2

1. Identify the main clause(s) in the following sentence:

   Oliver was worried that Karen's performance was deteriorating.

2. Identify the subordinate clause(s) in the following sentence:

   In fact, the last time he tried to escape, he ended up in the hands of the military police.

3. Is this a simple or a compound sentence?

   Joe's family loves seafood, and they order it twice a week.

4. Fill in the blank with the correct pronoun:

   People _____ live in gated communities are usually wealthy.

   (that, who, which)

5. Select the correct pronoun:

The statistics, _____ are provided by the government, are sometimes inaccurate. (that, who, which)

6. Are these compound or complex sentences?

   (a) The dog barked as Stacy rose begrudgingly from her chair.

   (b) Not knowing what his fate would be that day, Bob packed everything and stepped out the door.

7. Combine the following two sentences:

   The children were very polite. We saw them yesterday.

8. Combine the following sentences into a periodic sentence.

   I was shopping in Dubai last week. I met Olivia.

Chapter 4

How to Improve Your Writing Style

Writing style refers to how you package your written work. It distinguishes outstanding prose from average writing. Since you want your work to be widely accepted, even though such recognition comes with time, getting the basics of writing style right will greatly help you.

Since we have not looked at the use of grammar in your sentences, it is prudent to look at it now because grammar is at the core of fundamentals of writing.

How to Improve Your Grammar

This section reviews two basic grammar rules you need to write correct sentences. These are subject-verb agreement and pronoun-noun agreement. Let's look at these rules in more detail.

1. Subject-verb agreement: A verb should always agree with its subject.

Even with words between them, the subject and verb must agree. Here is an example:

> "The tutor [subject], as well as his pupils, was [verb] pleased with the test results."

When singular subjects are joined by "or"/"nor," use singular verbs; use plural verbs when plural subjects are joined by "or"/"nor." Consider the following:

> "Neither Esther nor her mother was pleased with the new promotion."

> "Neither the students nor the teachers are attending the party."

If you join a plural subject and a singular subject by the word "or"/"nor," let the verb agree with the subject closer to it.

Examples:

"Neither Esther nor her parents were pleased with the new promotion."

"Neither state workers nor the former governor is happy with the new government."

Words such as *anyone*, *nobody*, *everyone*, *somebody*, *anything*, etc. take singular words. Here is an example:

"Everyone was here yesterday."

2. Pronoun-Noun Agreement: Let your pronouns agree in person (she, they, it, etc.) and in number (plural or singular) with the noun to which they refer.

Pronouns must specifically refer to the noun they replace. Do not mix the third person "she/he/it" with second person "you."

Examples:

Avoid...

"To improve one's chances of getting a job, you have to go to school."

Use...

"To improve your chances of getting a job, you have to go to school."

"To improve <u>one's</u> chances of getting a job, <u>one</u> has to go to school."

Use apostrophes to indicate contraction or possession. Add an apostrophe after the owner word to show possession. However, there is no need to have an "s" after an apostrophe if the word ends in a double or triple "s."

Examples:

"I saw one boss' car."

"I saw many bosses' cars."

Also, avoid using an apostrophe for plurals of regular nouns.

Example:

"The students' left early." [No apostrophe should be used.]

Take time to sharpen your grammar skills. Write as much as possible, checking for and correcting consistent errors as you progress.

How to Add Flair

Equipped with basic knowledge of grammar and sentence structure, you can now work on improving your writing style. This can be done in four steps, each of which is described below.

Step 1: Choose an appropriate tone.

Your reader, the kind of assignment, and the purpose of your writing determine the level of formality you should use in your writing.

You may use the direct, personal, and simple informal tone or the formal impersonal tone, depending on your specific needs.

For an informal tone, use the active voice as much as possible since you are likely to be employing a more casual form of writing. The informal tone works best for journal entries, or informal class work. It resembles well-organized conversational speech, without clumsy pauses or excess slang or colloquialisms.

On the other hand, the formal tone is used more often for writing longer, more complex sentences. It also may also involve the use of specialized, abstract vocabulary and appears most often in essays and academic papers. While using a formal tone, avoid pompous phrases, clumsy structures, or excessive verbiage.

Irrespective of the tone you use, you must be direct, clear, and comprehensible.

Step 2: Do not use the passive voice unless it is necessary.

Always remember that the active voice involves an actor acting on an object or receiver (e.g., "Paul kicked the ball."). Conversely, the passive voice involves the object or receiver being acted upon by an actor (e.g., "The ball was kicked by Paul.").

The active voice keeps your writing conversational, allowing your reader to connect with your thoughts at every moment. The active voice implores your reader to take action or helps them easily visualize an action taking place.

The passive voice, on the other hand, is best used in contexts where emphasis is placed on procedures and processes during which human agency is minimized. Use the passive voice to give an account of how you or someone else did something only when the identity of the actor is not as important as the effect, reception or result of an action.

Step 3: Make your writing simple, concise, and precise

Aim to communicate your point as concisely as possible to minimize strain on your readers. For instance, to convey a similar meaning, you may opt for a shorter word rather than a long one. Moreover, limit the use of unnecessary words. Use the word "about" instead of verbose expressions like "with regard to," "in reference to," etc. Moreover, avoid the use of empty passive phrases like "it was found that," "it is recommended," etc.

Using overused words or expressions and clichés will not make your work better. Use words such as "case," "situation," "factor," "aspect," and "position" sparingly so that your writing does not become vague. Furthermore, avoid using ambiguous expressions and terms. For instance, to show a relationship of time, use the word "while/when" instead of "as."

Step 4: Avoid beginning sentences with "There is" Or "There are."

The word "there" is an expletive. Such a word may serve a function at times but lacks meaning. Always restructure your sentences to avoid using needless words.

Example:

"There are five balls on the table."

The word "there" in this sentence is unnecessary. In rewriting the sentence, you get:

"Five balls are on the table."

Starting a sentence with the pronoun "this" or "that" can also make your writing vague or hard to follow. You should only use "this/that" when referring directly and clearly to a noun in the preceding sentence. Further, you should not use "this/that" to refer to a whole paragraph.

Consider the following example:

> "A student's work has no value unless she shares her thoughts with her tutor. That is the beauty of education."

In this case, the pronoun "that" makes the sentence unclear. The previous sentence has very many subjects, and your reader must guess what "that" specifically refers to.

As you practice writing in different formats, be consistent with your writing style. To sharpen your skills, read extensively and intensively.

Now, let's recap what we just learned. Take the quiz below, trying your best to answer the questions to see if you grasped this chapter's key points.

Quiz 3

1. Complete the following sentences with the right word(s):

   a. One of his brothers ¬___ going ¬___ a trip ___ Canada.

   (is, on, to; are, on, to; is, to, for)

   b. The lady with the little dog ___ on our street.

   (live, lives)

   c. The secretary, together with the chairman, ___ the congregation ___.

   (greet, cordially; greets, cordial; greets, cordially)

2. Rewrite the following sentences without beginning with "There."

   a. There is a bee in my porridge.

   b. There is an old radio in the living room.

   c. There are twelve months in an ordinary year.

3. Correct the following sentences:

   a. She practiced fishing, swimming, and to hunt.

   b. As she's the instructor, we should listen to her.

4. Simplify the following sentences:

   a. There are problems with the Church.

   b. There is a natural desire among teenagers to experience freedom from their parents.

CHAPTER 5

More Ways to Turbocharge Your Sentences

Now that you understand the various sentence types of sentences, the parts of sentences, and a few ways to improve your writing, you are ready to move on to learning additional techniques to turbocharge your sentences. In Chapter 5, we look at four techniques you can employ to take your writing to the next level: (1) Avoid nominalizations; (2) be concrete/specific; (3) choose the right word; and (4) add a dash (or two).

1. Avoid nominalizations

A nominalization is a verb or adjective disguised as a noun. For example, *act* is a verb and its nominalized form is *action*; similarly, *happy* is an adjective and *happiness* is its nominalized counterpart. Using words like "action" or "happiness" in sentences is not usually a problem. Problems do arise, however, when *-tion*, *-sion*, *-ness*, or *-ment* nouns are used too frequently.

The first way nominalization weakens your writing is that it adds excess words to your sentences. Brevity is a key feature of good writing, but it is hard to be concise with too many nominalizations in sentences. Consider the sentence, "He is the kind of person who exhibits passion." Compared to "He is passionate" it is too wordy. The latter sentence in fact says the same thing but one-third of the words. That makes it preferable.

The second problem with too many nominalizations is that they make sentences boring and difficult to read. Consider, for example, "At lunch time the consumption of sandwiches by my classmates and I occurred while we held a discussion on the perils of climate change." This sentence without nominalizations would simply read: "At lunch time my classmates and I ate sandwiches and discussed the perils of climate change." The first sentence is dull and verbose, while the revised version is to the point and easy to follow.

The technique here is just to avoid using too many nominalizations. Try to substitute the original verb or adjective in place of the noun cluttering up the sentence to make your writing more vigorous and captivating.

2. Be concrete/specific

A key feature of poor or lackluster writing is that it is vague or lacks specificity. Usually the problem is that the writer has not included enough details for the reader. Consider the two examples below.

> Example #1: "Last week a man died at a park."

This sentence does not tell readers when exactly the man died, how he died, where he died (other than "a park"), what his name was (if known), and other details that may be important.

> Example #2: "On Saturday, July 9, 2016, John L. Kramer, aged 58, of 231 Green St. in Smithville was struck and killed by lightning while jogging in Morgan Park."

The second example, a sentence like one would find in journalistic writing, provides specific details so that readers can know exactly what happened to the man, who he was, and what he was doing at the time of his death. While every detail about the incident cannot be included in one sentence, the second example sentence does not leave the reader with too many unanswered questions.

A related error novice writers make is to use abstract language where concrete language would be more effective. Consider the next two examples.

> Example #1: "Ted quickly perceived that the used car salesman was dishonest."

This sentence does not appeal to any of the five senses—sight, hearing, taste, touch or smell. As such, the reader will have trouble visualizing what Ted perceived and why he reached his conclusion.

> Example #2: "To Ted, the used car salesman's greasy hair, whiskey breath, tacky yellow suit, and clammy handshake immediately indicated he was not someone to be trusted."

The second sentence appeals to the reader's sense of smell ("whisky breath"), sight ("yellow suit," "greasy hair"), and touch ("clammy handshake"), painting a vivid and memorable scene for the reader. The reader will also be able to understand why Ted perceived the salesman was dishonest.

3. Choose the right word

English, like any other language, has many general all-purpose words that can be readily used in conversation. They are often among the first words a child will learn. Words like "happy" or "sad" are examples of two such adjectives. Among such verbs are "walk," "talk," "throw," "jump," and so on. To better convey a feeling, thought or action with such words speakers will simply add an adverb. Thus, a person can feel "very happy" or "very sad." They can also "walk slowly," "talk loudly," etc.

This is not so bad in conversation, for which general language will usually be sufficient. In fact, if a person is too eloquent in their everyday speech it can sound odd or possibly pretentious. Writing differs, however. When a writer uses simple words like "happy" or "sad" the reader will feel that the word choices are too vague or general.

To better understand how important choosing the right word is consider the examples that follow.

> Example #1: "John walked slowly toward the door."

This sentence contains no errors per se, but it is weak because it does not precisely indicate how John was walking, other than to add "slowly."

Example #2: "John shuffled toward the door."

Here, John "shuffled," which is a type of slow walking. An elderly person might shuffle. "Shuffled" is thus more specific than "walked slowly."

Example #3: "John strutted toward the door."

In the third example, the verb "strut" is used. "Strut" implies that John is proud or possibly vain in some way. Someone who thinks they are attractive or are proud of some achievement might "strut." Thus. "strut" again reveals more than just "walk slowly."

The principle described above also applies to adjectives. Let's look at a few examples with "happy" and "sad."

Example #1: "Janet felt very sad after Tim broke up with her."

Example #2: "Janet was heartbroken when Tim broke up with her."

Example #3: "Michael was very happy when he heard he was accepted into Harvard University."

Example #4: "Michael was thrilled to hear he was accepted into Harvard University."

Examples #1 and #3 both use the basic words "happy" and "sad" with the modifier "very." "Very" is itself an empty word that adds nothing to a sentence's meaning. "Happy" and "sad" are also too simple and general to convey emotions found in specific contexts. "Heartbroken" better describes Janet's feelings after her break-up as does "thrilled" better describe Michael's feelings after learning he was accepted into Harvard University.

4. Add a dash (or two)

The dash can be used in place of parentheses, commas, semicolons, or colons. It can be used to introduce lists, add additional information, or amplify a thought. The dash is also helpful for adding variety and punch to writing. Let's examine a few ways you can add a dash (or two) to your sentences.

> Example #1: "I like fruits such as apples, oranges, peaches, and pears because they are sweet."
>
> Example #2: "I like fruits such as apples, oranges, peaches, and pears—anything sweet."

In Example #2, the writer adds "anything sweet" at the end of the sentence to clarify why he likes certain fruits. Example #1 conveys the same idea and is fine, but Example #2 sounds more informal and punchier.

> Example #3: "It's my pizza, so don't eat it."

> Example #4: "It's my pizza—don't eat it."

Example #3 clearly states that the pizza belongs to the speaker and he or she does not want the listener to eat it. Example #4 says the same thing, but putting the dash before "don't eat it" stresses those three words and amplifies the speaker's feelings about the pizza.

> Example #5: Steven's girlfriend—the rich one who drives a Porsche and plays soccer—works at Goldman Sachs.

This example sentence employs dashes to offset extra information about Steven's girlfriend. Parentheses or commas would also work, but dashes allow the information to not be downplayed (as with parentheses) or interrupt the flow of the sentence (as commas would in this case).

> Example #6: "The pantry was stocked with junk food—soft drinks, potato chips, cookies, cake, and all kinds of candies."

In Example #6 the dash is used before a list, in this case of junk foods. A colon would also work but would give the sentence a more formal feel.

The thing to remember when employing the dash is to not overuse it. Like any technique, it will lose its effectiveness if used too often. Used sparingly, however, the dash can add impact and variety to paragraphs.

And that completes Chapter Five. To see how well you have grasped the ideas we have covered try the quiz on the following page.

Quiz 4

1. Rewrite the following sentences without nominalizations:

> *a. We reached the conclusion that the study was not feasible.*
>
> *b. There is opposition among my neighbors toward the government's recycling policy.*
>
> *c. I had a feeling of pleasure when I learned I received 100 percent on my exam.*

2. Rewrite the following sentences so they include more specific details.

> *a. The food at the restaurant tasted good.*
>
> *b. I enjoyed the movie.*
>
> *c. Frank wore nice clothes on his date with Nancy.*

3. Replace the bold words with a precise verb or adjective in the following sentences:

> *a. Frederick looked quickly at his watch. He had only been jogging for 3 minutes.*
>
> *b. Sonia spoke quietly into my ear so no one else could hear.*

c. I was very happy when I won the lottery.

4. Rewrite the following sentences using dashes.

   a. My best friends, Anne, Murray, Leo, and Peter, have all moved away.

   b. I need three items from the grocery store. I need milk, eggs, and butter.

   c. You look pretty in that dress. You are absolutely stunning.

CHAPTER 6

Some Additional Stylistic Tips

Avoiding common mistakes, whether in grammar or usage, is one strategy you can employ to help you craft well-constructed sentences. However, this strategy alone is insufficient to make your sentences truly turbocharged. Beyond knowing what pitfalls to avoid, you should also familiarize yourself with stylistic devices you can employ to further engage your intended audience. This chapter provides five tips on how to use such devices to turbocharge your writing: (1) Hype it up (hyperbole); (2) Amp it Up (amplification); (3) Play it down (understatement); (4) Create a clash (antithesis); and (5) Be bold, brash, and boisterous (alliteration).

1. Hype it up (hyperbole)

Hyperbole is a figure of speech that refers to an exaggerated statement or claim not meant to be taken literally. Common in everyday conversation, it is also used in writing to emphasize a sentiment or emotion. Very often, hyperbole produces a humorous effect. Below are three examples of hyperbole in action:

> Example #1: "When I saw all the Fs on my report card I knew one thing: Mom would kill me. My life was over."
>
> Example #2: "The music was so loud I thought my head would explode!"
>
> Example #3: "Frank Miller is a mountain of a man."

In the first example, the writer exaggerates what he/she expects his/her mother's response will be like to a report card with Fs. The writer could say something like, "Mom would be very disappointed and was going to be hard on me from now on." However, this version lacks the humor and intensity of the sentence using hyperbole.

The writer in the second example does not literally mean his/her head almost exploded. Readers will understand this exaggeration to mean that the music was VERY loud, not just "loud" as normally understood.

Mountains are immense natural formations that are far larger than any living thing, including a man. Thus, to say that Frank Miller is "a mountain of a man" suggests he is very, very large. Just saying that Frank is "very large" lacks the impact of the phrase "mountain of a man."

---

2. Amp it Up (amplification)

Like hyperbole, amplification is a rhetorical device writers use to emphasize an idea. Amplification differs from hyperbole, however, in that it consists of details that are added to a sentence to make it more intriguing, entertaining or intense. Consider the following two examples of amplification:

Example #1:

"Sophie was beautiful to behold—her face radiated like the countenance of an angel; her hair resembled braids of shimmering gold; and her eyes glinted like the azure seas of the French Riviera."

Example #2:

"Anne felt sick that morning as the packed train she was on left Grand Central Station. Her lungs wheezed, her head throbbed, and her throat ached. Worse yet, she felt herself beginning to heave; to her horror, she realized was about to throw up the bacon and eggs she had eaten for breakfast."

In both examples above, the main idea is intensified through additional details. To show just how "beautiful" Sophie was to her admirer the first sentence refers to images of angels, gold, and the sea. This is more effective than just saying Sophie was "very beautiful." In Example #2, the reader can determine just how sick Anne felt on the train by noting her symptoms, feelings, and reactions. The fact that she was on a crowded train is another detail that makes the situation seem more anxiety-laden to the reader.

3. Play it down (understatement)

While hyperbole can serve as an effective rhetorical device in certain contexts, in others the writer can use understatement to his or her advantage. With this device, the writer appears to minimize the importance or significance of a situation to inject a sense of irony, sarcasm or surprise into a passage.

> Example #1: "As the packed train left Grand Central Station, Anne, unable to move her arms or hands amongst the mass of people pressing on her, sensed she was about to vomit. 'Wonderful,' she thought. 'Just wonderful.'"
>
> Example #2: "My boss is not the friendliest person you'll ever meet."
>
> Example 3: "Warren Buffett knows a thing or two about investing."

Anne in Example #1 would be expected to be having a "terrible" day as she is sick and about to vomit on a packed train. However, she thinks, "Wonderful. Just wonderful," revealing an unexpected viewpoint to the reader. Here, the writer uses sarcasm to show that the day began in a disastrous way for Anne. In the second example the writer could have just said, "My boss is a cold, unfriendly person," but by using understatement the same idea is conveyed in a more restrained and sophisticated way. Most people know that US businessman Warrant Buffett is considered one of the greatest investors of all time. To say he "knows a thing or two" about investing, as in Example #3, relays this fact in a subtle yet humorous way.

4. Create a clash (antithesis)

Antithesis is a rhetorical device that includes opposing ideas in a sentence to achieve a contrasting effect. Making skillful use of parallelism, antithesis is a powerful tool that skilled writers use to produce memorable, elegant, and quotable sentences.

> Example #1: "Ask not <u>what your country can do for you</u>, but <u>what you can do for your country</u>." —John F. Kennedy

> Example #2: "That's one <u>small step for man</u>, one <u>giant leap for mankind</u>." —Neil Armstrong

> Example #3: "It was the <u>best of times</u>, it was the <u>worst of times</u>, it was the <u>age of wisdom</u>, it was the <u>age of foolishness</u>." —Charles Dickens, A Tale of Two Cities

Most educated readers are familiar with all three of these quotations. Imagine how different each would sound expressed without antithesis. "Americans should do more for their country" and "This step I am taking is significant for mankind" are hardly memorable. Likewise, *A Tale of Two Cities* would not be *A Tale of Two Cities* without the antithesis Dickens used to begin his literary masterpiece. Such is the impact of antithesis on the written and spoken word.

5. Be bold, brash, and boisterous (alliteration)

Alliteration is a stylistic literary device that repeats identical or similar sounds at the beginning of successive words, as in the title of this sub-section. Through alliteration writers can prompt readers to focus on a specific passage as well as add color and variety to their prose.

> Example #1: "Sammy the snake smiled and snored as he slept soundly."
>
> Example #2: "The bashful businessman bored Betty with his banal banter."
>
> Example #3: "Laura loved Larry and Leonard but loved the latter a little less."

Read the three example sentences aloud and note the effect. Although alliteration is common in literature it also appears in advertising and business contexts. Well-known company names based on the device include Bed Bath & Beyond, Best Buy, BlackBerry, Dunkin Donuts, Krispy Kreme, LuluLemon, and Chuckee Cheese. Most people are also familiar with such products as Coca Cola, KitKat, Tetley Tea, TicTacs, and Planter's Peanuts.

The stylistic tips described in this chapter, like others mentioned in this book, should be used selectively for maximum impact. With regular practice, they will come to mind naturally at the right time for you to use to keep your readers focused on your message. Let's now try another quiz to help you retain what you have just learned.

Quiz 5

Identify the stylistic devices used in the following sentences.

1. "It's just a flesh wound!" (said by a knight in Monty Python's *In Search of the Holy Grail* after his arms and legs have been severed by King Arthur's sword)

a. Alliteration
b. Understatement
c. Antithesis
d. Amplification
e. Hyperbole

2. "We waited for an eternity for the concert to begin."

a. Alliteration
b. Understatement
c. Antithesis
d. Amplification
e. Hyperbole

3. "[F]or the twenty million of us in America who are of African descent, it is not an American dream; it's an American nightmare. —Malcolm X

a. Alliteration
b. Understatement
c. Antithesis
d. Amplification
e. Hyperbole

4. "*Veni, vidi, vinci* [I came, I saw, I conquered]." —Julius Caesar

a. Alliteration
b. Understatement
c. Antithesis
d. Amplification
e. Hyperbole

5. "America has given the Negro people a bad check, a check which has come back marked 'insufficient funds'." —Martin Luther King, Jr.

a. Alliteration
b. Understatement
c. Antithesis
d. Amplification
e. Hyperbole

Conclusion

As you can see, good writing—or *writing right*—consists of numerous facets that interact with and support one another. It is often thought that certain people have a "gift" with writing that others cannot replicate. However, it should be apparent from this guide that enthusiasm, knowledge, and practice offer a means for average writers to improve their skills to the point they can write turbocharged sentences that captivate, persuade, and effectively inform readers, whatever their needs and backgrounds.

By improving your writing, you stand to reap multiple rewards. Through exceptional writing, you can develop your analytical skills and enhance your intellectual capacity. You can also greatly improve your job and income-earning prospects. In our era of globalization, your influence as a skilled writer could even reach audiences in other world regions. Anything is possible with good writing! It's not just written communication either. What you can express on paper, you can also express orally. The higher the quality of your words, the more powerful your communication will be and the greater will be your impact.

I hope this book helped you understand how to turbocharge your writing to help you attain your career and life goals. The next step is to implement everything you have learned.

All the best in your future writing endeavors!

Answers to Quizzes

Quiz 1

1. The modifiers are: "Poor" (adjective), "who just wanted a quick meal" (adjective phrase), "to get her through her two-hour botany lab" (infinitive phrase), "on the floor" (prepositional phrase), "as a spider crawled out" (adverb phrase)," and "from under her lunchbox" (prepositional phrase).

2. The modifier phrase is "with a jaunty, defiant step, as if daring passersby to intrude upon her cheerful mood."

3. Once his paper was corrected and rewritten, he excelled.

4. After frying the burgers for 30 minutes, we turned the cooker off.

5. The correct answer is "b." The participle phrase "Filling the shopping basket with bottled water and canned foods" precedes "we," its logical target.

6. The correct answer is "a." Answers "b." and "c." contain misplaced modifiers. In "b.," Mary is "squeaky with rust" and in "c." it is the park that is "squeaky with rust."

7. Yes. "With an ear-to-ear grin," a prepositional phrase, describes the test, but its target should be the tutor. The sentence should read: "With an ear-to-ear grin, the tutor returned the Mathematics test to a delighted Emily."

8. a. They found him at the beach; b. The police apprehended the culprits; c. Who taught you French?; D. People from the South started the revolution.

9. The passage has no fragments.

10. This is a run-on sentence. Put a full stop between "4:20 pm" and "make" so that the result reads as follows:

> "The meeting begins at 4:20 pm. Make sure you arrive early."

Quiz 2

1. "Oliver was worried."

2. "In fact, the last time he tried to escape."

3. A compound sentence.

4. Who/that.

5. Which.

6. a) compound; b) complex.

7. The children that we saw yesterday were very polite.

8. When I was shopping in Dubai last week, I met Olivia.

Quiz 3

1. a. is, on, to; b. lives; c. greets, cordially.

2. a. A bee is in my porridge.; b. An old radio is in the living room; c. An ordinary year has twelve months.

3. a. She practiced fishing, swimming, and hunting; b. Because she's the instructor, we should listen to her.

4. a. The Church has problems; b. Teenagers naturally crave freedom from parents.

Quiz 4

1. a. We concluded that the study was not feasible; b. My neighbors oppose the government's recycling policy; c. I was pleased to learn I received 100 percent on my exam.

2. Note: Answers will vary. a. The lunch buffet at Wang's Chinese Restaurant was superb and reasonably priced; b. The acting and sets in the remake of "The Great Gatsby" were remarkable for

their realism; c. From his perfectly-coiffed hairstyle to his Giorgio Armani suit and Gucci shoes, Frank resembled a dashing Hollywood actor on his date with Nancy at Le Bernardin, New York's most exquisite restaurant.

3. a. Frederick glanced at his watch. He had only been jogging for 3 minutes; b. Sonia whispered into my ear so no one else could hear; c. I was overjoyed/thrilled/ecstatic when I won the lottery.

4. a. My best friends—Anne, Murray, Leo, and Peter—have all moved away; b. I need three items from the grocery store—milk, eggs, and butter; c. You look pretty in that dress—absolutely stunning.

Quiz 5

1. b.

2. e.

3. c.

4. a.

5. d.

Printed in Great Britain
by Amazon